UPCYCLE IT!

Crafts for Kids

Fun and Useful Projects to Recycle and Reimagine

JENNIFER PERKINS

For Ages
8 to 12

ROCKRIDGE
PRESS

For general information on our other products and services or to obtain technical support, please contact our Customer Care Department within the United States at (866) 744-2665, or outside the United States at (510) 253-0500.

Rockridge Press publishes its books in a variety of electronic and print formats. Some content that appears in print may not be available in electronic books, and vice versa.

Interior and Cover Designer: Jennifer Hsu
Art Producer: Melissa Malinowksy
Editor: Mary Colgan
Production Editor: Ruth Sakata Corley
Production Manager: David Zapanta

Photography © 2021 Elysa Weitala, cover and pp. iii, 2, 8, 16, 22, 24, 28, 32, 36, 42, 44, 48, 52, 56, 62, 64, 68, 72, 76, 82, 84, 88, 92, 96; © 2021 Jennifer Perkins, pp. 3, 4, 6, 7, 10, 11, 14, 15, 18, 19, 23, 26, 27, 30, 31, 34, 35, 38, 39, 43, 46, 47, 50, 51, 54, 55, 58, 59, 63, 66, 67, 70, 71, 74, 75, 78, 79, 83, 86, 87, 90, 91, 94, 95, 98, 99. All illustrations used under license from Shutterstock. Author photo courtesy of Jennifer M. Ramos.

Paperback ISBN: 978-1-63807-132-7
eBook ISBN: 978-1-63807-527-1
R0

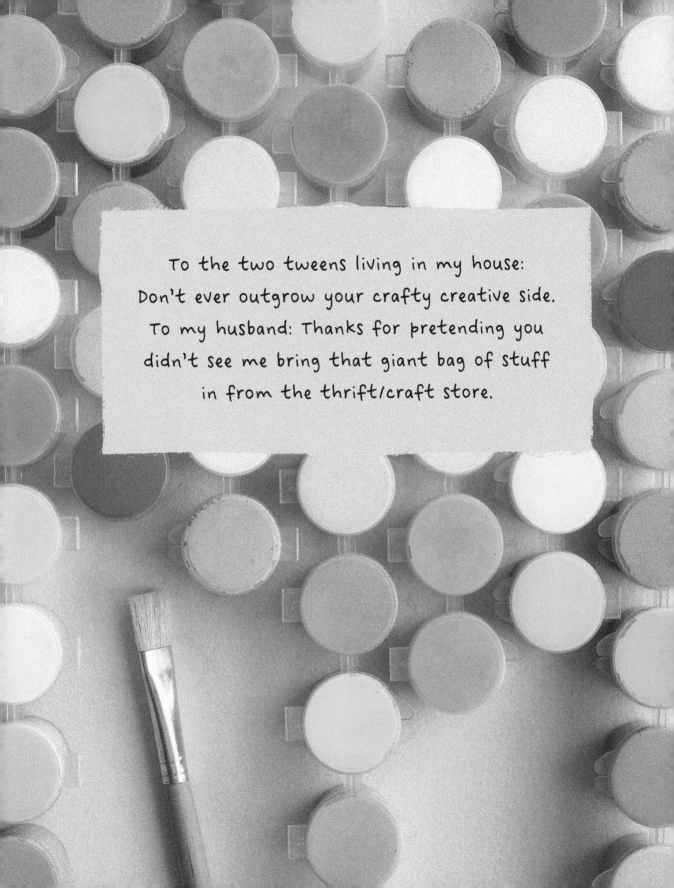

To the two tweens living in my house:
Don't ever outgrow your crafty creative side.
To my husband: Thanks for pretending you
didn't see me bring that giant bag of stuff
in from the thrift/craft store.

Contents

Welcome to Upcycled Crafting

Hi, my name is Jen, and I'm a quirky craft-loving lady from Austin, Texas. I got my start crafting as a kid, just like you. My first "serious" venture into the world of crafting was with a pair of earrings I entered in the science fair when I was in fourth grade. One earring was a tube of toothpaste; the other was a travel-size toothbrush. They dangled so long you could almost wear them and brush your teeth at the same time—brilliant! Fortunately, I decided to leave teeth cleaning to the dental professionals, while I became a creative professional. I have done advertising campaigns for Michaels (the arts and crafts store), worked on TV shows and videos for HGTV, and written craft books—this is my third. Isn't that cool? You really can grow up to be a crafter. I'm the proof!

Read carefully, because I am about to tell you one of the best secrets to my success: You don't need to go to a craft store and spend a lot of money to make creative magic. If you have glue and scissors, you are good to go. Start looking around your house for inspiration, and be sure to take a look in the recycling bin. What does "upcycled" mean? Upcycling is all about taking something that is no longer useful and giving it a new purpose. That ripped T-shirt? It is a rug waiting to be made. Last night's spaghetti jar? A pen holder with style. Once you start seeing old objects in new ways, you're ready to get crafty.

This book has 25 ideas, all inspired by items that have been thrown away. With all the possible variations on these projects, there are more than 100 craft concepts here. The book is organized into five themed chapters: organizers for your things, room decorations, fun school supplies, super-cool stuff to wear, and creative gifts to give to friends and family. All of these projects are not only cool to look at (Hello, cactus lamp!) but they are also useful (Hello, no more banging your shin on the corner of your bed thanks to that cactus lamp.). Most of the projects are low mess and can be whipped up in under an hour. Check the Messy Meter level at the top of each craft for a number of dots from 1 to 5, with 1 dot being the least messy and 5 dots being the messiest. You will learn the basic crafting skills to create a storage container out of straws, decorate a tote bag with a potato, and organize your pens and pencils with an old sock and a plastic bottle. Each project in this book has easy-to-follow instructions, plus an advanced crafting idea if you want to take the project further. Puzzle-piece pottery and scented crayons are as useful as they are unique—and fun to make.

My hope is that you will walk away from this book feeling inspired to take on all kinds of craft projects. You can use these ideas and techniques as a springboard to come up with your own projects. And as a bonus, your upcycling efforts will be helping the environment, one craft project at a time.

Getting Started

When you start seeing the world through upcycled, splatter-painted glasses (see page 62), everything becomes a crafting opportunity. Take the ideas in this book and tweak them with your own variations. Just because the craft shows an ice cream cone potato stamp, it doesn't mean you can't use a banana shape. This is your book now, so make the crafts your own. And remember, the sky is the limit on what you can upcycle. Oops—scratch that. Your parents set the limit, so be sure to ask their permission before you start gluing toys to their favorite picture frame or cutting up their yoga mat to make a door sign.

There is no right or wrong way to get started. The crafts are grouped by theme, but there is no strict order to them. Feel free to jump around and do whatever craft you like. Start at the front of the book, skip to the middle, or jump ahead to the last project. Wherever you begin, have fun and let your creativity flow! You may come across terms and craft items you are not familiar with. Less-familiar terms and items appear bold in the text, and a description of them is provided in the glossary at the back of the book.

Materials to Upcycle

You can't save everything from the recycling or garbage bin, hoping that an item might one day come in handy for a craft. But do keep an eye out for things that have a lot of potential, like a pair of jeans that no longer fit but would look great as a journal cover, or a large piece of cardboard that could be turned into coat hangers. You might want to flip through all the crafts in this book, pick out some projects you want to tackle, and take note of what supplies you will need. Have you almost finished the oatmeal? Then remind your parents to save the container so you can cover it with paper straws. Are there only two eggs left in the carton? Well then, you are just two eggs away from making yourself some spiffy new string lights.

Here is a list of crafty items to keep an eye out for and to hang on to when you find them:

» Jars with interesting shapes
» Tie-dye T-shirts
» Picture frames
» Broken crayons
» Small toys
» Single socks

Essential Tools and Supplies

There are a number of craft items that are great to always have on hand. Many of these items can be found at a large retail store or craft store. If you really want to keep up with the environmental theme of this book, ask your parents to find out if you have a Buy Nothing group in your neighborhood. Several materials I used in this book, such as broken crayons, cardboard containers, and glass jars, were dropped off on my porch, free of charge. All I had to do was ask.

Cardboard
The possibilities for cardboard in crafting are endless. Hold on to old shoe boxes, toilet paper rolls, and shipping boxes, and you'll always have plenty when inspiration hits.

Craft glue
A bottle of all-purpose craft glue is a crafter's best friend. It's stronger than school glue, dries clear, and can be used on all kinds of materials, like paper, wood, plastic, and fabric.

Craft paint
There's no need to buy expensive paint when you can get a full rainbow of colors for less than a dollar a bottle.

Hot glue
Hot glue dries faster than craft glue and is great for materials that are hard to glue, like the egg cartons in "Egg-cellent String Lights" in chapter 2.

Paintbrushes
You don't need to look for fancy paintbrushes. Most craft stores have inexpensive packages that come with several sizes and bristle shapes.

Pom-poms
A bag of multicolored pom-poms is great for embellishing any craft.

Scissors
You'll want something a little sturdier than round-tip school scissors for most of these projects. Ask your parents if there's a spare pair to keep with your crafting supplies.

Safety Note

CAUTION

Keep an eye out for the caution symbol throughout the book. This symbol means an adult should help you with, or supervise, one or more of the instruction steps. Sharp objects like scissors and needles can pierce your skin, and hot glue can burn you. Also, make sure you always use glue and paint that are labeled safe for kids—in other words, no toxic chemicals. Look for the AP (approved product) seal on containers.

Upcycling Tips & Tricks

One of the best parts about crafting, especially with recycled materials, is that there is no right or wrong way to make something. No two projects will ever look exactly alike, and that is what makes them so special.

Here are some tips to keep in mind as you enter the world of upcycled crafting:

1. Don't become a hoarder (someone who keeps everything). Sometimes having too many supplies can become overwhelming. Save just a few things at a time—glass jars this week, soda bottles next week.

2. Keep your work area clean. A clean workspace is more inviting. Also, keeping your work area clean will make it more likely your parents will support your crafting enthusiasm. Use old newspapers or drop cloths to protect surfaces, and put your supplies away when you are finished using them.

3. Don't be discouraged by a lack of supplies. If you don't have green hot glue, use green paint to color cooled glue dots instead. Is the silicone baking mold you found round instead of rectangular? Awesome! You'll make round crayons.

4. Always take care of your supplies. Rinse out your paintbrushes thoroughly, make sure to close the glue properly, and unplug the hot glue gun when you're done to avoid injuries.

5. Make sure to start with clean materials. That means no bits of yolk in your egg cartons or dried pasta sauce at the bottom of the jar. Wash materials with soap and water before starting.

6. Your projects are not going to look like the projects in the photos, and that's terrific! Everyone's work is unique, and your projects are going to reflect who you are. What if your project doesn't turn out perfectly? That's okay. Things don't have to be perfect, and you can always try the craft again. Your skills will only get better and better.

7. Check in with your community. My town has a craft supply thrift store where you can fill an entire bag for five dollars. You can also ask your parents about Buy Nothing groups on Facebook.

8. Feeling festive? Many of these projects can be tweaked into holiday or party décor. For example, make werewolf hangers instead of cute cats, or birthday balloon-shaped confetti crayons.

9. Don't be afraid to mess up. Remember, most of your supplies came out of the recycling bin. If your project doesn't turn out the way you hoped, just pop it back in the bin and start again.

10. Pat yourself on the back for doing your part to help the environment. Every little bit helps.

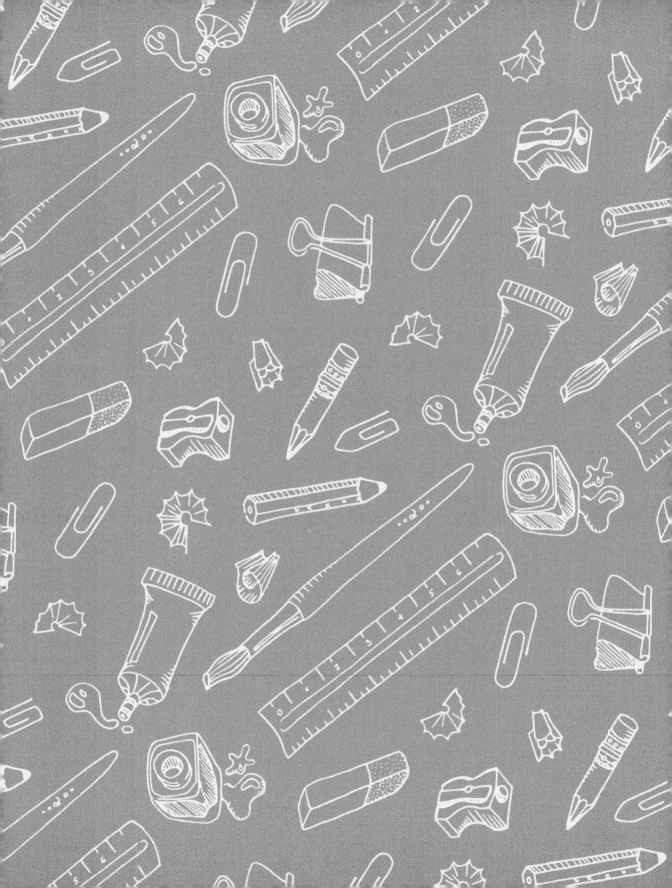

CHAPTER 1

Organize Your Things

"A place for everything and everything in its place" is something many of us hear when we're kids. Would you be more likely to hang up your clothes if the hanger was a smiling cat? Would you keep your desk tidier if your pen holder was rainbow colored? You are going to have a lot of fun finding out if fancier, upcycled storage materials help you keep your room neat. Grab some paper straws and empty cereal boxes—it's time to get crafty and get things organized!

Cute Critter Cardboard Hangers

Picking up your clothes and hanging them in the closet is going to be a lot more fun with animal cardboard hangers.

What You Need

Clothes hanger
Cardboard
Pen
Scissors
Craft paint
Paintbrush

What You Do

1. Place the hanger on the piece of cardboard and trace around it with a pen. Do not trace the hook (the part that goes over the closet rod).

2. Draw the shape of an animal's head where the hanger hook would go. You can draw a cat (like in the photos), a dog, a lion, or even a dragon—whatever you like. These critter hangers are so easy to make, you can create an entire zoo!

3. Draw the shape of a hanger hook coming from the top of the animal's head.

4. Carefully cut out the entire shape. You may need an adult's help with this, because cutting cardboard can be difficult.

5. Use craft paint to paint the animal's face with the paintbrush. If the paint you are using is not very thick or the cardboard has printing on it, you may need to paint the cardboard white first. Let the paint dry completely before adding details.

ADVANCED CRAFTING
Cardboard hangers are probably not strong enough to hold a heavy jacket. To make a sturdier hanger, draw the hanger shape twice and glue the two pieces of cardboard together.

Top-Notch Tip
When you draw the shape of the hanger hook, be sure to take the size of the closet rod into consideration.

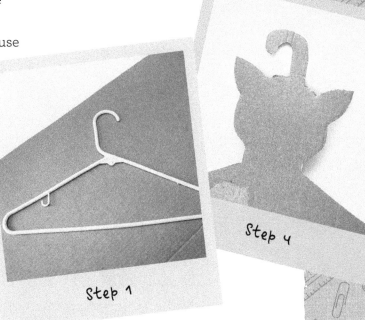

Step 1

Step 4

Jazzy Jars

Organize your pens and pencils in style. You will never put another glass jar in the recycling bin once you see how awesome they look with a quick food coloring make-over. The finished jars make great gifts, too.

What You Need

Glass jars
Decoupage medium
Food coloring
Craft sticks
Drop cloth (optional)

Step 3

Step 4

What You Do

1. Make sure the glass jars are completely clean and dry. Some labels leave a sticky residue when they are removed, so a jar might need to be soaked in warm, soapy water to get it all off.

2. Fill each jar with about 2 inches of decoupage medium.

3. Add 10 to 20 drops of food coloring to each jar. If you want the color to be darker, add more drops. If you want the color to be lighter, add fewer drops.

4. Stir well with a craft stick. The food coloring should be totally blended into the decoupage medium, without streaks.

5. This step can get messy, so get an adult to help you, do this outside, or spread out a drop cloth. Roll the tinted decoupage medium around in the jar until the entire inside surface is evenly coated.

6. In a sunny area outside, turn each jar upside down with the mouth balanced on 2 craft sticks. This will allow the decoupage medium to drain out.

Step 7

Top-Notch Tip

Remember how colors mix: yellow and blue make green, red and blue make purple, and yellow and red make orange. Use a basic food coloring set to create almost any color you want.

7. Allow the jars to dry for up to 24 hours. There may be drips around the mouth of the jar, which you can easily trim off with scissors.

ADVANCED CRAFTING

Try using more than one color in the same jar. Using one color at a time, mix the decoupage medium and food coloring in a separate container, then pour it down one side of the jar. Pour out the excess on the same side. Then do the same with the next color. Allow drying time between colors and repeat until the entire inside of the jar is striped with different colors.

Cereal Box Notebook Holder

They say breakfast is the most important meal of the day. When it comes to craft supplies, that might be true! Next time you finish a box of cereal, get crafty with this clever notebook holder.

What You Need

Cereal box
White paint (optional)
Paintbrush (optional)
Cardboard (optional)
Ruler
Pen
Scissors
Craft glue or **decoupage medium**
Wrapping paper

Step 2

Step 3

What You Do

1. Optional step: Most wrapping paper is fairly thin. If you want to make sure the print and pictures on the cereal box don't show through the paper on your finished project, paint the cereal box white before you begin. Set the box on a piece of cardboard and allow the paint to dry completely before you start step 2.

2. Lay the cereal box on a table. Use a ruler to draw a diagonal line from the center of the left side of the box to the upper right corner.

3. Cut off the top flaps of the box. Then cut out the triangle shape you created with your diagonal line.

4. Use the triangle you just cut out as your guide to mark off a second triangle on the other side of the box. Cut out the second triangle.

5. Cut off the narrow side of the box so that the bottom corners of the triangles on each side are lined up.

Step 5

Top-Notch Tip

No wrapping paper? No problem! You can paint your boxes, cover them with **washi tape**, or glue on pictures from magazines. How you decorate your boxes is entirely up to you.

6. Coat the cereal box with a thin layer of craft glue or decoupage medium. Wrap the box with wrapping paper just as you would wrap a gift. Trim and fold the paper, smoothing out bubbles and wrinkles as you go.

7. Optional step: Use as many cereal boxes as you want for this project. Then, using craft glue, attach the finished cereal boxes to each other on their sides. Adding a cardboard base will help make the boxes stable. Cut a piece of cardboard to fit the bottom of your cereal box notebook holders. Then cover it with wrapping paper and glue it to the bottom of the boxes.

ADVANCED CRAFTING

Think beyond cereal boxes. This same idea could be used with large boxes to create a storage box for toys or a laundry hamper. A round canister could be turned into a fancy holder for your comb or brush.

Mini Memo Board

Now that you are getting organized, you are going to need a place to post reminders, school pictures, lists, and more. All you need is an old picture frame and some fabric and ribbon to make a marvelous mini memo board.

What You Need

Large picture frame
2 sheets craft felt
Craft glue
Ribbon
Scissors

Step 1

Step 2

What You Do

1. Make sure your craft felt sheets are the same size as the inside of your picture frame. Trim them, if necessary. Remove the glass from the frame and set it aside for another craft project.

2. Use craft glue to attach one sheet of felt to the picture frame backing.

3. Lay 3 strips of ribbon diagonally across the picture frame backing. Make sure the 3 strips of ribbon are equally spaced apart. Glue the ends of the ribbons to the other side of the frame backing.

4. Repeat step 3, going in the opposite direction with the ribbon to create a crisscross pattern. The crisscross pattern of the ribbons will be what holds your items to the memo board.

5. Put the picture frame back together.

6. Cut a piece of ribbon that is about 5 inches longer than the width of the memo board. On the back side of the frame, glue one end of the ribbon to each top corner. This ribbon will be used to hang the memo board.

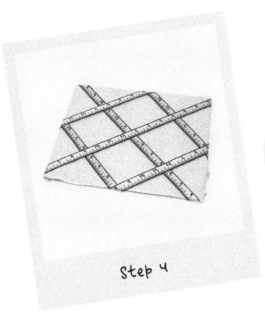

Step 4

Top-Notch Tip

Instead of felt, you can use any type of fabric, such as an old T-shirt, a cloth napkin, or a pillowcase. The material just needs to fit in the frame. Likewise, instead of ribbon, you can use yarn or twine.

7. Cover the back of the frame with the second piece of craft felt using craft glue.

8. Hang your mini memo board in a convenient place in your room.

ADVANCED CRAFTING

Is one memo board not enough for all your items? Add a second one by repeating steps 1 to 5. Then glue 2 short pieces of ribbon to the back of the bottom 2 corners of the first memo board and the back of the top 2 corners of the second board, so the second board hangs below the first one.

Simple Straw Storage Container

Combine a bunch of colorful paper straws and a recycled cardboard container, and what do you get? Your new favorite desk storage item.

What You Need

Empty cardboard canister (from oatmeal, grits, bread crumbs, or similar)
Paper straws (enough to cover the entire outside of the container)
Ruler
Scissors
Craft glue
Large-eye plastic needle
Yarn (bright color)

Step 1

Step 3

What You Do

1. Measure the height of the card-board container. Cut the paper straws to the same height.

2. Using craft glue, attach the straws to the outside of the card-board container. Allow the glue to dry completely.

3. Thread a large-eye plastic needle with colorful yarn. Starting at the bottom of the container, go up through one straw and out through the top. Then bring the yarn down to the bottom outside the straw. Take care to line up the yarn between the straws.

Step 4

Top-Notch Tip

If you don't have paper straws, you can make your own by rolling colorful magazine pages, junk mail, or construction paper into straw-shaped tubes. After rolling the paper, fasten the end to the tube with craft glue. Once the glue on your tubes has dried, you can cut them to the size of your cardboard container.

4. Repeat step 3 with the next straw, and go all the way around the container. Tie off the ends of the yarn when you are done.

ADVANCED CRAFTING

Add trim to the top the container, such as a row of pom-poms. This trim can help hide slight differences in straw height. Allow the glue on the trim to dry completely.

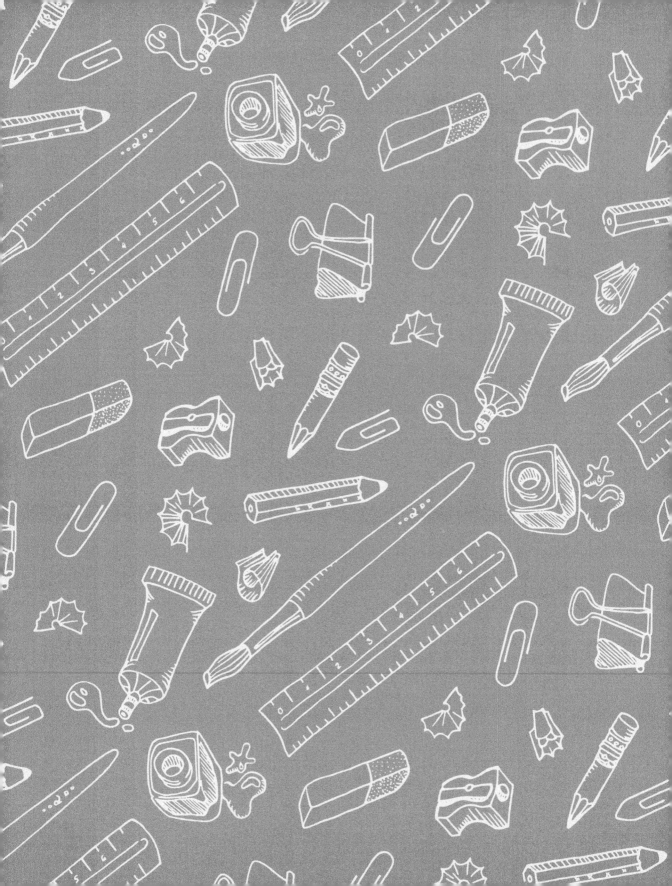

CHAPTER 2

Decorate Your Room

It is time for you to get in touch with the interior decorator inside you by using egg cartons, hot glue, and yoga mats. In this section, you are going to add some personal touches to your space with the help of a door hanger and a new mini floor mat. All you need is a green bottle and an old tie-dye shirt to get started. If you share a room with a sibling, include them in the crafty fun, too. After all, the only thing better than one plastic bottle cactus lamp is two plastic bottle cactus lamps. Do you have a jigsaw puzzle with missing pieces taking up space in your closet? No one wants to do a puzzle with pieces missing, so turn the ones you have into a one-of-a-kind bedside bowl.

Crafty Cactus Night-Light

CAUTION

This unique cactus night-light combines "going green" with having a green thumb. No watering or sunlight is required, just a battery change now and then.

What You Need

Empty green
  2-liter bottle
Scissors
Hot glue gun
Green hot glue
Tap light or LED candle
Terra-cotta pot
Double-sided
  tape (optional)
Pom-pom

What You Do

1. Remove the label from the bottle, then wash and dry the bottle.

2. Use the scissors to cut off the top part of the bottle. Cut below where the bottle begins to become narrower. The opening at the top of the bottle should be slightly smaller than the top of the terra-cotta pot. Ask an adult for help cutting the bottle if you find it difficult.

3. Using the green hot glue, make small dots all over the bottle. These dots are the cactus spines. Do one area at a time. Let the glue dry before turning the bottle, to prevent dripping.

4. Place a tap light or LED candle at the bottom of the terra-cotta pot.

5. Insert the green bottle "cactus" in the terra-cotta pot. If the bottle does not stay upright, secure it to the inside rim of the pot with double-sided tape.

6. Glue a pom-pom on top of the bottle for an extra pop of color. Instant cactus flower!

ADVANCED CRAFTING
Add an extra level of realism to the cactus spines with toothpicks. Cut off the pointy tips of several toothpicks. While the hot glue dots are still wet, insert the toothpicks into the glue.

Top-Notch Tip
If you do not have green hot glue, try using green dots of paint to make the cactus spines (puffy paint works great).

Step 2

Step 4

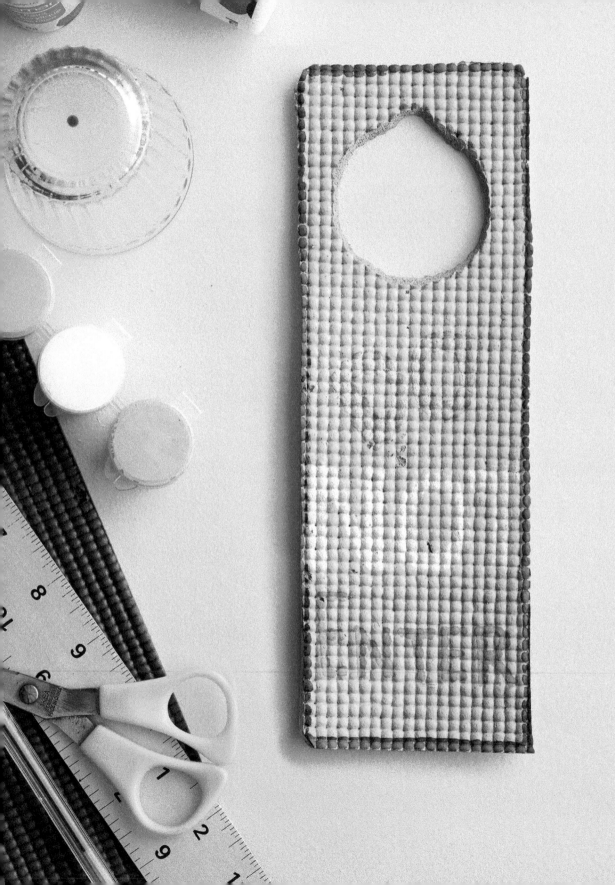

Let Your Door Hanger Do the Talking

Do you want to welcome people into your room—or keep them out? This do-it-yourself door hanger will do the trick.

What You Need

Old yoga mat

Ruler

Drinking glass

Pen

Scissors

Multi-surface craft paint, any color

Paint markers

Step 1

Step 3

What You Do

1. Cut off a small section from an old yoga mat. Make sure it's larger than 9 by 3 inches. Wash it well with soap and water, then let it dry completely.

2. Use the ruler to draw a 9-by-3-inch rectangle on the piece of mat.

3. Place the glass upside down near the top of the rectangle and center it between the two long sides. Trace all around the glass to create a circle.

4. Use the scissors to cut out the rectangle. Then cut out the material inside the circle. The round hole will be where the door hanger goes over the doorknob.

5. Paint the door hanger with the multi-surface craft paint. Allow the paint to dry completely.

6. Use the paint markers to write a message on the door hanger, such as "Do Not Enter" or "Homework in Progress."

Step 6

Top-Notch Tip

If you do not have an old yoga mat you can upcycle, it's not a problem. You can make a door hanger from almost any material that is easy to cut and slightly stiff, even thick cardboard.

7. Repeat steps 5 and 6 on the back of the door hanger. Write a different message there, such as "Come On In!" or "Welcome!"

ADVANCED CRAFTING

Take the design of your door hanger up a notch with some embroidery. Yoga mats are made from a foam material that can be easily punctured. With a needle and yarn, or embroidery floss, you can add a fancy blanket-stitch edge to your door hanger and make it even more impressive.

Egg-cellent String Lights

CAUTION

Did you just eat the last egg? Don't toss the carton away. Use it to light up your room in a fun, upcycled way, with egg carton string lights.

What You Need

Egg cartons
Scissors
LED string lights
Hot glue gun
Hot glue
Pom-pom trim

Step 1

Step 4

What You Do

1. If you are using a Styrofoam egg carton, wash it with soap and water, then let it dry completely. If you are using a cardboard egg carton, wipe it as clean as you can with a dry cloth.

2. Use the scissors to cut apart the egg carton. You may need to trim the edges of each egg cup a bit. Cut out as many egg cups as there are lights. If you have more than 12 lights, you will need more than 1 egg carton.

3. Use the tip of the scissors to make a small hole in the top of each egg carton cup. This will be where each bulb of the string lights goes into the egg carton "lamp shade."

4. Insert a light bulb into each hole you made in the egg carton cups. Place a small amount of hot glue around the hole so the egg carton lamp shade stays in place.

Step 5

Top-Notch Tip

Styrofoam egg cartons come in some fun colors, but cardboard egg cartons can be painted any color you like.

5. Decorate the egg carton lamp shades with pom-pom trim. Cut sections of trim to the correct size and use the hot glue to attach it around the edges of each lamp shade.

ADVANCED CRAFTING

Egg cartons have been a favorite item of upcycling crafters for many years. Have fun searching online for egg carton crafts and see what you can find. Get inspired and try making some of the crafts you discover.

Puzzle Piece "Pottery"

CAUTION

Okay, puzzle pieces are not exactly like pottery, but when you put enough of them together to make a jazzy bowl, they sure look like it. Do you have a jigsaw puzzle that is missing some pieces, or one you are just done with? Now you have a clever use for it.

What You Need

Jigsaw puzzle pieces
Hot glue gun
Hot glue
Craft paint
Paintbrush (firm and narrow)
Decoupage medium

Step 4

Step 6

What You Do

1. Gather your puzzle pieces. The size of your bowl will depend on how many puzzle pieces you have. The bowl in the photos was made using about 300 pieces. Feel free to mix and match pieces from different puzzles, as long as the pieces are similar in size.

2. Lay out a selection of puzzle pieces on a flat surface. The pieces should touch each other, but not overlap. These pieces will be the base of your bowl.

3. Use the hot glue to attach a puzzle piece on top of two base pieces to connect them.

Continue with more pieces until the entire base of the bowl is solid.

4. Start building out the sides of your puzzle pottery by gluing stacks of puzzle pieces around the circumference (outside edge) of the bowl. Glue the pieces just as you did for the base.

5. Once the bowl is the depth you want, begin to create the lip of the bowl by gradually extending the puzzle pieces outward.

6. When the bowl is the shape you want, turn it over and add extra hot glue in random spots to make sure the bowl is sturdy.

UPCYCLE IT! CRAFTS FOR KIDS

Step 7

Top-Notch Tip

Skip the paint job. The random colors and patterns of the puzzle pieces create a one-of-a-kind work of art.

7. Use the craft paint and a firm paintbrush to paint the entire surface of your bowl. Your paintbrush should be narrow enough to reach into the crevices between the puzzle pieces. Make sure not to be too generous with the paint, as too much paint might warp the cardboard pieces.

8. Let the paint dry completely. Afterward, coat it with a thin layer of decoupage medium to seal it.

ADVANCED CRAFTING

Make a perfectly round puzzle bowl using a balloon. Balance a balloon on a dish. Cover half the balloon with puzzle pieces, gluing them in place with decoupage medium. Make sure each puzzle piece is touching other pieces at its edges. The decoupage medium will act as a glue and a sealer. When the decoupage medium has dried completely, pop the balloon and remove it. Now you have a perfectly round bowl.

T-Shirt Yarn Mini Rug

Do you love T-shirts? If you do, how would you like to step on one every day? This easy-to-make mini rug is the perfect use for T-shirts that no longer fit you. In fact, your new favorite rug may be in your dresser right now.

What You Need

T-shirts
Scissors
Ruler
Woven placemat or piece
  of **mesh canvas**

Step 1

Step 3

What You Do

1. Choose your T-shirt—the more colorful it is, the better! Old tie-dye shirts work great. Try to use shirts that don't have seams on the sides or anything printed on them. The rug in the photos was made from 3 T-shirts.

2. Using the scissors, cut off the bottom hem of the T-shirt.

3. Using the ruler, measure a band of material 2 inches high. Using the scissors, cut off the band from the bottom of the T-shirt. Then cut the band so it becomes one long strip.

4. Gently tug on each end of the strip. The jersey material will begin to curl in on itself, becoming more like yarn.

5. Repeat steps 3 and 4 until you have cut up the entire shirt.

6. Cut the T-shirt "yarn" into strips about 4 inches long.

7. Begin attaching the strips of T-shirt to the woven placemat or piece of mesh canvas by pulling the ends of each strip through two holes that are next to each other, from the back to the front of the placemat. Then tie the ends in an overhand knot on top.

Step 8

Top-Notch Tip

The more colorful the T-shirt, the more colorful the rug. Go for tie-dye, all-over-print styles, and even stripes. As long as the design is jersey and part of the material, that is, not printed on the T-shirt as an appliqué, you are good to go!

8. Continue tying on strips of yarn until the entire placemat is covered with T-shirt strips. The jersey material will make the half knots stay in place.

9. Trim the strips to roughly the same length while leaving the rug shaggy. Your new rug should be machine washable.

ADVANCED CRAFTING

If you can braid, you don't need a placemat. Try braiding long strips of T-shirt yarn, then coiling them into a circular or oval-shaped mat. Add a bit of glue as you go to hold the coils together.

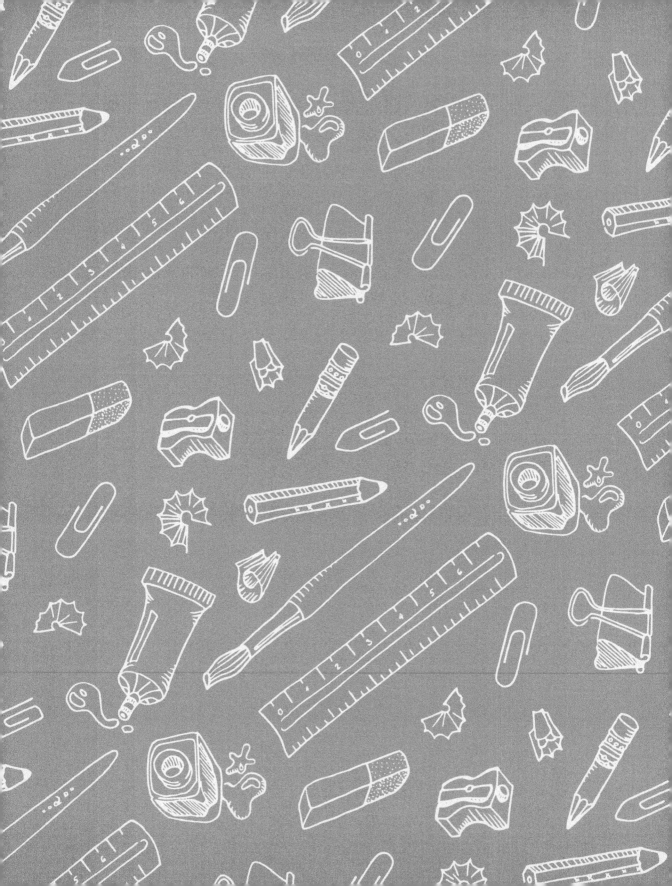

CHAPTER 3

Use It in School

School supplies are a big deal. Everyone wants to have the snazziest notebook or bookmark. In this chapter, you will make a few of your own supplies and ensure that they are extra cool for school. It is a sure thing that no one else in your class will have a pencil case made from the same sock and water bottle as yours. There's no chance of mixing things up at snack time when you are the only one with beeswax food wraps. That journal jacket made from your old jeans? It's totally your own fashion statement. Now, finish off that last granola bar and get ready to turn the box into a notepad.

Beeswax Food Wrap

CAUTION

Who has the most fun-looking lunch in the school cafeteria? You do, of course, with this clever do-it-yourself cling wrap. It is super easy to make. All you need is wax and fabric.

What You Need

Snack or sandwich
 container (or any
 favorite container)
Ruler
Cotton fabric
Pen
Scissors
Baking sheet
Aluminum foil
Natural beeswax pellets
Oven
Clean paintbrush

What You Do

1. Measure the opening of the container you want to cover. The fabric will need to be 2 to 3 inches larger than the opening of the container.

2. Trace the opening of the container on a piece of 100 percent cotton fabric. Add 2 to 3 inches on all sides, then cut out the shape.

3. Cover the baking sheet with aluminum foil. Lay the fabric on the foil-covered baking sheet. Cover the fabric with natural beeswax pellets.

4. You will need an adult's help with this step. Place the baking sheet in a warm oven; around 250°F works best. The wax will begin to melt almost immediately, so don't leave the baking sheet unattended.

5. Once the wax has melted completely, ask an adult to remove the baking sheet from the oven. If necessary, use a clean paintbrush to spread the melted wax so that it covers all the fabric. Allow the fabric to cool. Remove any excess wax from the edges of the fabric.

ADVANCED CRAFTING

To make your wrap more flexible, you can add a bit of **jojoba oil** to the melted wax. A good ratio is 1 tablespoon of oil per 1 cup of beeswax pellets.

Top-Notch Tip

The wrap may need to be refreshed every 2 to 3 months. When you see creases in the wax or notice that the wrap is not sticking as well as it used to, just heat it up again in the oven to remelt the wax.

Step 1

Step 3

Super-Easy "Laminated" Bookmarks

Did you know a roll of packing tape can be used like a laminating machine? This craft is so fast and easy, you will be making bookmarks for everyone. And not just bookmarks—the possibilities are endless.

What You Need

Colorful paper
Ruler
Scissors
Packing tape
Hole punch
Yarn

step 1

Step 3

What You Do

1. Choose the paper you would like to use for your book-mark and gather the rest of your supplies.

2. Most packing tape is about 2 inches wide. If this is the size of your tape, cut a rectangle of colorful paper 6 inches long by 2 inches wide. The paper should be the same width as the packing tape.

3. Cover the rectangle of paper with packing tape. Go slowly and try to avoid air bubbles

and creases. Do one side of the paper, then the other. The tape will act as lamination for your paper.

4. Using the hole punch, make one hole in the rectangle about ½ inch from the top.

5. Cut 11 pieces of yarn, each 3 inches long.

6. One at a time, loop 10 strands of the yarn through the hole in the rectangle and fold them over. The ends of the yarn should be even with each other.

Step 7

Top-Notch Tip

All kinds of paper work great for these bookmarks— wrapping paper, colorful magazine pages, and even old greeting cards.

7. With the 11th piece of yarn, gather all the folded loops of yarn at the top of the bookmark. Tie them tightly together to make a tassel. Trim the tassel to the desired length.

ADVANCED CRAFTING

Use your new laminating skills to make backpack or lunch box name tags. Just cover your homemade tag with tape, punch a hole in it, and tie it to your bag with yarn.

Jean Jacket Journal

Give your favorite journal a new look with a jean "jacket." The best part about this makeover? You gain a new pocket to hold pens and pencils.

What You Need

Old denim shorts or jeans
Scissors
Journal or notebook
Paintbrush
Craft glue
Craft felt or craft foam

Step 1

Step 2

What You Do

1. Cut the denim shorts or jeans from the waistband down past the zipper or button closure, all the way to the top of the thigh. Cut off the legs below the seat area. This should open up the shorts or jeans to create a single piece of denim.

2. Spread the denim on a flat surface with the outside of the pants facing down. Place the journal on the denim. Make sure to position the front of the journal so that the back pocket of the denim will be centered on the cover when the denim is turned over. Leave 1 or 2 inches of border around the journal and trim off the excess material.

3. Use the paintbrush to spread craft glue over the cover and spine of the journal. While the glue is still wet, wrap the denim around the cover, smoothing out any bumps.

4. Open the journal so you are looking at the inside front cover on the left. Before folding over the border of denim and attaching it to the inside cover, cut away a triangle of fabric for each of the four corners. The triangles should be almost flush with the corners. On the spine of the journal, trim away a small

Step 5

Top-Notch Tip

Jeans are not the only pants with pockets. Try using old corduroys, khakis, or even swim trunks. Anything with a pocket will do.

rectangle of fabric at the top and bottom.

5. Using the paintbrush, apply a layer of craft glue along the top, outer edge, and bottom of the inside cover. Fold the denim border over, onto the areas with glue. The rectangles and triangles you cut out should allow for sharp corners and edges at the folds.

6. Repeat steps 4 and 5 for the inside back cover.

7. Hide the rough edges of the denim on the inside front and back covers by gluing down craft felt or craft foam over the inside covers. Allow the felt or

foam to dry completely before closing your journal.

ADVANCED CRAFTING

Give your jean jacket journal some flair. Glue on decorative buttons, enamel pins, or embroidered patches.

Plastic Bottle Pencil Pouch

Who would have thought that a plastic bottle and a single sock would make the perfect combination? Well, they do—as a clever recycled pencil pouch.

What You Need

Plastic drink bottle
   (personal size)
Scissors
Long sock (hemmed at
   the top)
Craft glue
Rickrack, ribbon,
   or pom-poms
Cording

Step 1

Step 3

What You Do

1. Select a sock and gather the rest of your materials.

2. Cut off the top of the plastic bottle. Be sure to cut below where the curved part of the bottle stops. You might need an adult to help you. Throw the top half of the bottle into the recycling bin.

3. Cut the sock at the ankle. Throw away the bottom of the sock or save it for another craft.

4. Coat the top several inches of the bottle (near the opening) with craft glue.

5. While the glue is still wet, gently place the sock over the bottle, with the cut end at the bottom.

6. Use decorative trim, such as rickrack, ribbon, or pom-poms, to cover the cut end of the sock.

7. To create a casing for the drawstring closure, you will need 2 holes in the top, hemmed part of the sock. This will be where the 2 ends of the cording come out. Make 2 small slits close to each other in the hem of the sock, being careful not to cut through the top of the hem. The slits should have fabric at both ends.

Step 8

Top-Notch Tip
If you don't have cording for the drawstring on hand, an old shoelace works great, too.

8. Place the cording around the hem of the sock and through the 2 slits. This will be the drawstring closure.

9. Fold the hem of the sock over the cording. Glue along the edge where the hem touches the sock to create a casing for the drawstring. Allow the glue to dry completely.

10. Pull open the top of the sock and drop pens and pencils inside. When you have put in everything you need, pull on the drawstring and tie it tight to close up the sock.

ADVANCED CRAFTING
Feel free to take things a step further and embellish the bottom part of the bottle. You could make designs with permanent markers, glue the sock farther down so that very little bottle is showing, or glue on pom-poms to make polka dots.

Snack Box Notebook

CAUTION

Do you need a new notebook? Look no farther than your kitchen pantry. Grab an empty box, some sheets of paper, and get ready to learn how to bind a book.

What You Need

Cardboard snack box (from granola bars, fruit snacks, instant oatmeal, or similar)

Scissors

Paint

Paintbrush

6 sheets of paper

Binder clip, bobby pin, or paper clip

Ruler

Needle

Thread or embroidery floss

step 5

step 9

What You Do

1. The size of the box you use will determine the size of your notebook. If you want a large notebook, use a large box.

2. Cut off the top, the bottom, and 1 of the sides of the box. You should be left with what looks like a book cover—the front, the back, and the spine.

3. Using one of the box's creases, fold the box flat. Doing this will make one side longer than the other. Cut off the extra length so that the 2 sides of the box cover are the same size. Paint the cover and allow it to dry completely.

4. Fold the sheets of paper in half. Fold the box cover closed and lay it on a folded sheet. Trace the box to determine what size the sheet should be. Do this for each folded sheet. Cut all the sheets along the trace lines and set them aside.

5. Set the folded pages inside the book cover. Tuck 1 sheet inside the next, so the last sheet is tucked inside the other 5 sheets and the book cover.

6. Use a binder clip, bobby pin, or paper clip to hold the pages in place inside the cover.

Step 10

Top-Notch Tip
Use lined paper if you want to use your notebook for writing or blank paper if you want to use it for art. You could even use heavy watercolor paper to make a painting notebook.

7. To bind the notebook, you will do a 3-hole **pamphlet stitch**. Using the ruler, mark 3 evenly spaced dots on the center fold of the book with a pen or pencil. Poke a hole through each dot with the needle. You may need an adult's help with this.

8. Thread the needle with the thread or embroidery floss and knot the end.

9. Push the needle through the middle hole from the outside, leaving a long tail of thread.

10. Pull the needle through the middle hole from the inside. Push the needle out through the top hole. Bring the needle down along the folded edge (the spine) and push it through the bottom hole. Bring the needle up on the inside and push it out through the center hole. Tie the 2 pieces of thread together, tightening any slack. Trim off the extra length of thread. Now you have your own homemade notebook.

ADVANCED CRAFTING
The folded section of sheets inside your notebook is called a *signature*. Try adding more signatures to your notebook to give yourself more pages.

CHAPTER 4

Create Your Own Style

Style is a very personal thing. Maybe you like to blend in with the crowd. That's cool. Or maybe you like to always stand out from the crowd. That's cool, too! Whatever your preference is, you can take the craft ideas in this chapter in the direction that best suits you and your style. Are pink flamingos too much for your earbud holders? No big deal. **Washi tape** comes in more subtle designs. Do you love the idea of trying **shibori** dyeing, but you are not a big fan of blue? Swap out the indigo-colored dye for lime green or hot pink or whatever color you choose. And what better way to customize your accessories than with some potato stamping? Yes—potatoes!

Splatter Paint Sunglasses

Are you bored with last summer's sunglasses? Give them an easy makeover with the help of craft paint. Splattered paint never looked better.

What You Need

Large-framed plastic
  sunglasses
Washi tape (or painter's
  tape)
**Multi-surface
  craft paint**
Disposable cup or plate
Water
Small paintbrush
Newspaper (optional)

What You Do

1. Cover the lenses of the sunglasses with washi tape.

2. Pour a small amount of multi-surface craft paint into a cup or onto a plate. Add a couple of drops of water and mix well.

3. Place the sunglasses on a sheet of newspaper or take them outside to minimize any messes. Load a small paintbrush with paint and run your finger over the tip of the brush to splatter the paint onto the sunglasses. You can also use a short swatting motion with the paintbrush, which will flick paint onto the sunglasses.

4. If you want to splatter a second color, make sure to let the first color dry completely. This will prevent the splattered paint from getting too thick and running.

5. Let the final color of paint dry completely, then remove the washi tape.

6. Try on your cool, new sunglasses and get ready to show them off.

ADVANCED CRAFTING
Take things up a notch by gluing rhinestones to the corners of the sunglasses, trimming the frame with a chain, or even adding tiny toys across the tops of the lenses for something extra funky.

Topnotch Tip
Instead of splattering the paint, try creating different patterns, such as stripes, squiggly lines, or spots.

Step 1

Step 3

Awesome Earbud Case

CAUTION

Do you like chewing gum? With this craft, you can transform the plastic chewing gum container into a nifty earbud case, faster than your gum loses its flavor.

What You Need

Small round plastic
  chewing gum or
  mint container
Washi tape
Wax paper
Circle shape to trace
Pen
Scissors
Needle
Jump ring
Pliers
Carabiner or key chain

Step 1

Step 2

What You Do

1. Remove the label from the plastic container and gather the rest of your materials. You may need to soak the container in warm, soapy water to remove the last sticky bits of the label. Let the container dry completely.

2. Apply washi tape to the wax paper in strips. Make sure you line up the pieces close together and have enough to cut out 2 circles that will be slightly smaller than the size of the plastic container.

3. Using a circular-shaped item, such as a glass or cup that is slightly smaller than the container, trace a circle onto the wax paper covered with washi tape. Do this twice, so that each side of the container has a circle of washi tape.

4. Cut out the 2 circles from the wax paper. Then cut each circle in half.

5. Gently peel the half circles of washi tape from the wax paper. Apply them to the plastic container, lining up the straight edges along the opening of the container.

Step 4

Top-Notch Tip

Gum and mint containers come in various shapes and sizes. If you don't have a round container, you can use a square or rectangle one instead. Follow the instructions for decorating with washi tape, but trace something square or rectangular on the wax paper instead of something round. It's the same concept, just a different shape.

6. Ask an adult to help you poke 2 holes into the side of the plastic container with a needle. The holes should be roughly the width of the jump ring.

7. Using pliers, thread the jump ring through the hole in the container and squeeze it closed. Attach a carabiner or key chain to the jump ring.

ADVANCED CRAFTING

What else could be turned into a small earbud case? An empty pill jar or even a dental floss dispenser can get a washi tape makeover and become a stylish little storage container.

Recycled Rolled Up Paper Beads

Old magazines can be turned into a unique key chain with this easy technique for making paper beads. Once you get "on a roll," you won't want to stop.

What You Need

Magazine

Scissors

Ruler

Straw

Glue stick

Bamboo skewer

Paintbrush

Decoupage medium

Cording, yarn, or twine

Plastic beads

Jump ring

Key chain

Step 2

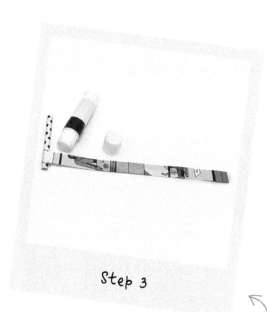

Step 3

What You Do

1. Choose a magazine page full of colors and patterns. You will see only small bits of each color and pattern once you start rolling the beads, so make sure the magazine page has as much variation as possible.

2. Cut 4 strips from the magazine page. Each strip should be slightly narrower than the one before. Use the ruler to measure them, if necessary. Cut the narrowest piece into a long triangle shape so one end finishes with a point. (If you want a thick bead, cut out more strips. Just make sure the strips get gradually narrower.)

3. Starting with the widest strip, roll the strip tightly onto a straw. Occasionally add a bit of glue to hold the strip in place.

4. Using the glue stick, attach the second, slightly narrower strip to the center of the first strip. Roll the strip around the straw.

5. Repeat step 4 with the third and fourth strips. Allow the glue to dry completely.

6. Once the glue has dried, slide the bead off the straw or trim the straw to the size of the bead and leave it in place.

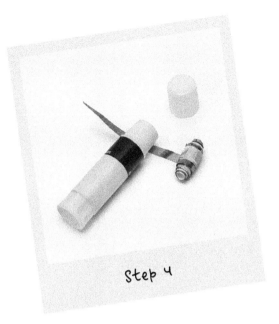

Step 4

Top-Notch Tip

Want to paint your paper beads? Once you have made all the beads you want for any project (key chains, necklaces, garland), you can use craft paint to paint the beads any color or pattern you like.

7. Repeat steps 2 to 6 to create as many beads as you want.

8. Thread the beads onto a bamboo skewer, then rest the ends of the skewer on 2 objects so the beads are elevated. With the paintbrush, coat the beads with a thin layer of decoupage medium. Allow them to dry completely.

9. Cut a piece of cording, yarn, or twine. On the cording, thread a plastic bead, a paper bead, and then another plastic bead. Loop the cording through the **jump ring** on the key chain, then thread it back down through the top plastic bead, the paper bead, and the bottom plastic bead. Tie a knot with the 2 ends of cording to create a tail.

10. Repeat step 9 for as many beads as you want the key chain to have. Vary the lengths of the cording and mix up the colors to add more interest.

ADVANCED CRAFTING

Paper beads can be created in a variety of shapes and sizes. Search for "recycled paper beads" online and take a look at the many patterns that come up. Try your hand at creating these slightly more complicated variations.

Stylish Potato Stamping

Potatoes are not only good to eat, they are also a handy craft supply. Upcycle an old bag (or a piece of clothing) with a stamp-endous new design!

What You Need

Potato
Knife
Cookie cutter
Paper towel
Scrap cardboard
Drawstring bag
Paintbrush
Multi-surface craft paint
  or fabric paint

Step 1

Step 2

What You Do

1. Ask an adult to help you cut the potato in half. Use the size and shape of the cookie cutter to determine whether to cut the potato lengthwise or crosswise.

2. Press the cookie cutter into 1 of the potato halves about halfway.

3. Ask an adult to help you cut away the potato from around the outside edge of the cookie cutter. Do not cut away the potato completely. Leave enough potato, with skin on the back, so you can easily handle the potato.

4. Remove the cookie cutter. Blot the potato dry with a paper towel to remove excess moisture.

5. Place a piece of cardboard inside the drawstring bag and inside any pockets in the bag. This will prevent paint from seeping through the bag from one side to the other.

6. Using the paintbrush, apply multi-surface craft paint (or fabric paint) to the potato. If your stamp will have 2 colors (like the ice cream cone in the photos), apply both colors to the potato before stamping.

Step 8

Top-Notch Tip

Potato stamps are great for creating designs on paper, too. Try creating your own wrapping paper using sheets of newspaper or brown paper bags.

7. Decide what pattern you want to create on the drawstring bag. Position the potato stamp, then press it firmly onto the bag. Make sure you make good contact with the stamp on the fabric. Pull away the potato to reveal the stamp image.

8. Repeat as many times as you like. Be sure to apply fresh paint to the potato stamp each time. If you want to change the colors, use a paper towel to remove the previous colors of paint from the potato.

9. Use the paintbrush to make any needed touch-ups to the stamp images. Allow the stamped bag to dry completely.

ADVANCED CRAFTING

Feel free to decorate the stamp images further. Finishing touches like hand-printed sprinkles on ice cream, googly eyes on a dinosaur, or a glitter glue outline are all great ideas.

Tie-Dye Shibori Bag

Give an old bag a new look with the Japanese tie-dyeing technique called **shibori**. Traditionally, this technique uses indigo (blue) dye. It offers unlimited options, depending on the fold you choose, and it works well with craft store dye.

What You Need

Small white bag,
  100 percent cotton
Craft sticks
Rubber bands
Navy blue dye
Drop cloth (optional)
Rubber gloves

Step 2

Step 4

What You Do

1. Make sure that the bag you plan to dye is 100 percent cotton. Also, if you are going to dye something that is new, you will need to wash it first because most new items contain **sizing**, which will not take dye.

2. This variation of shibori requires a simple accordion fold. Starting at the bottom of the bag, begin folding the bag, placing a craft stick between each fold as you go.

3. When you reach the top of the bag, secure the folds and sticks tightly with rubber bands.

4. Mix the navy blue dye according to the package instructions. Take the bag and the dye outside to a grassy area or spread out a drop cloth. Wearing rubber gloves, apply the dye to the accordion folds on both sides. Apply just enough dye to cover the areas so you do not see any white. Be sure *not* to apply too much dye.

5. Allow the dye to dry overnight.

6. When the dye has dried, remove the rubber bands and craft sticks.

Step 6

Top-Notch Tip

Try this tie-dyeing technique on T-shirts, scarves, or even bedsheets. As long as the fabric is 100 percent cotton, it will absorb the dye. Also, there is no need to use only navy blue. This technique will work with any color in the rainbow.

7. The bag should look striped at this point. To get a checkered pattern, repeat the accordion fold technique, this time going from one side of the bag to the other, instead of from bottom to top as you did before. Secure the folds and sticks with rubber bands.

8. Again, apply the dye to the edges of the bag that are showing, but do not apply too much. Allow the dye to dry overnight.

9. When the dye has dried, throw away the craft sticks and rubber bands. Wash the bag (do not wash anything else with it) and allow it to dry.

ADVANCED CRAFTING
Look up the Japanese art of shibori dyeing online to learn more about it. The accordion fold used here is a crafty interpretation of the many intricate and beautiful traditional techniques that involve items like poles and pies, and even stitching.

CHAPTER 5

One-of-a-Kind Gifts

The next time you need to come up with a gift for someone, skip going to the store and instead sort through the recycling bin. Who wouldn't want an adorable trinket dish made from an old newspaper, or colorful crayons that smell as good as they look? Even if you have bought the perfect gift already, you can still go for sustainability by wrapping the gift with reusable paper. Now, find an old scratched-up record (your grandparents probably have one), and let's rock around the clock with these fun projects that are perfect for gift giving.

Reusable Gift Wrap

The next time you are preparing to wrap a gift, try your hand at the Japanese art of **furoshiki**. The gift recipient will not only love their present, but they will also be able to regift the fabric wrapping.

What You Need

Square of fabric large
   enough to wrap the
   gift box
Square gift box

What You Do

1. Lay the fabric flat on a table.

2. Place the gift box in the center of the fabric.

3. Fold 1 side of the fabric over the box. Tuck the edge of the fabric under the box.

4. Fold the other side of fabric over the box. Tuck the edge of the fabric under the box.

5. Bring 1 of the 2 remaining sides of fabric toward the center of the box, creasing it in at the corners.

6. Repeat with the last side of fabric.

7. Tie the 2 sides together in a knot at the top. Make sure not to tie the knot too tight. The knot should be loose enough to be untied fairly easily, so the fabric can be used again.

ADVANCED CRAFTING
Use fabric markers, tie-dye, or other techniques from this book, such as potato stamping or **shibori**, to make your own furoshiki cloths out of plain white fabric.

Topnotch Tip
Bandannas and scarves work great for furoshiki, but almost any fabric will work. For small gifts, try using cloth napkins. For larger gifts, you can cut out pieces of fabric from old clothing or bedsheets.

Step 2

Step 3

Scented Marble Crayons

CAUTION

These crayons smell as good as they look. By working some magic on a bunch of broken crayons, you will create a feast for the eyes and the nose.

What You Need

Crayons
Scissors
Cookie sheet
Aluminum foil
Oven-safe rectangular
  baking mold
Oven
Timer
Essential oils

Step 2

Step 5

What You Do

1. Remove the paper wrappers from the crayons. The easiest way to do this is to use a scissors blade to cut a slit in the wrapper; ask an adult to help you with this. Once it is slit, the wrapper should come off easily.

2. Separate the crayons into groups of similar shades. For instance, gather all the reds and pinks together, all the shades of blue together, and so on.

3. Break the crayons into small pieces.

4. Line the cookie sheet with a piece of aluminum foil. This will protect the cookie sheet from any spilled wax. Place the baking mold on the cookie sheet.

5. Fill each cavity of the baking mold with pieces of crayon almost all the way to the top.

6. Preheat the oven to 250°F. When the oven is ready, ask an adult to place the cookie sheet inside the oven and set the timer for about 15 minutes. Ovens vary, so check the mold occasionally. Look to see when the crayons have melted and there are no longer pieces of crayon visible.

Step 9

Top-Notch Tip

It's important not to shake the baking sheet too much when removing it from the oven. This could make the wax colors blend together and become muddled.

7. Ask an adult to remove the cookie sheet from the oven.

8. While the crayon wax is still liquid, add 2 or 3 drops of essential oil to each individual mold. Try to match scents with colors, like adding lemon oil to the yellow wax and pine oil to the green wax.

9. Allow the wax to cool and harden completely. Remove the new crayons from the mold. (Remember, once the baking mold has been used to melt crayons, it should no longer be used for food.)

ADVANCED CRAFTING

The only thing better than a scented crayon is a scented crayon candle. Using an oven-safe glass jar, place a candlewick inside and fill the jar with broken crayons. Set the jar on a foil-covered cookie sheet. Have an adult help you with the oven and melt the crayons at 250°F. Allow the melted wax to cool and harden, then trim the wick.

Newspaper Trinket Dish

Yesterday's newspaper can become a trinket dish once you learn how easy it is to make paper clay. Use the dish to hold nonfood items, such as jewelry or coins.

What You Need

Newspaper, at least
  20 sheets
Small disposable bowl
  or container
Water
Craft glue
Paintbrush
Scissors
Decoupage medium
Craft paint

Step 4

Step 7

What You Do

1. Tear the sheets of newspaper into small pieces; the smaller the better.

2. Fill the disposable bowl (or container) with the torn newspaper.

3. Add enough water to the bowl to cover all the newspaper.

4. Add about 2 tablespoons of craft glue to the water and stir with the handle of the paintbrush.

5. Allow the mixture to sit for several hours. Stir the mixture occasionally and add more water, if necessary. The newspaper should begin to break down into a pulpy consistency. The pulp is ready when it has the consistency of clay and can be shaped. This is your paper clay.

6. Remove the paper clay from the bowl. Flip the bowl over and start covering it with the paper clay. Squeeze the paper clay slightly before applying it to the bowl. Continue to squeeze the paper clay as you apply it to remove excess water and help mold it into shape. Cover the bowl completely, so there are no gaps or holes.

7. Set the covered bowl aside and allow the paper clay to dry out. This step may take a couple of days, depending on the

Step 10

Top-Notch Tip

Instead of newspaper, you can use shredded printer or binder paper. You may need to use hotter water and let the paper soak a bit longer to create the same consistency of paper clay that is created with newspaper.

humidity where you live. If the weather is warm and sunny, set the bowl outside to speed up this step.

8. Once the paper clay has become hard to the touch, gently remove it from the bowl. It should hold its shape on its own. If the paper clay bowl is uneven, use the scissors to trim around the edge.

9. Apply a coat of decoupage medium to the inside and outside of the bowl as a sealant.

10. Use craft paint to decorate the bowl. Allow the bowl to dry completely.

11. When the paint has dried, apply a second coat of decoupage medium to seal the paint.

ADVANCED CRAFTING

What else could you make with paper clay? The answer is . . . almost anything! You could create small sculptures, beads for jewelry making, or even bigger bowls, using an inflated balloon as the mold. Let your imagination be your guide.

Rockin' Around the Record Clock

Okay, so vinyl records are making a comeback. But some records are too scratched up to be saved and listened to. Time for you to get creative and bring new meaning to "rockin' around the clock."

What You Need

Vinyl record (album size)
Paintbrush
Craft paint
Ruler
White marker
Number stencils (1 to 12)
Stencil brush
Clock hardware
Batteries

Step 2

Step 3

What You Do

1. Paint over the center label of the record with craft paint. Allow the paint to dry completely. If you would rather see the center label on the finished clock, skip this step.

2. Using the ruler and white marker, make 12 marks around the outer edge of the record. Be sure the marks are evenly spaced.

3. Place the 12 stencil numbers in their correct positions. Use the stencil brush to paint all the numbers. Allow the paint to dry completely.

4. Once the paint has dried, peel off the stencils. Use the paint-brush and a bit of paint to tidy up the edges of the numbers, if necessary.

Step 5

Top-Notch Tip

If you prefer a smaller clock, use a 7-inch record. Look for a 7-inch record that has the same small hole in the center as a full-size record. Some 7-inch vinyl records have large holes in the center that might be too big for clock hardware.

5. Follow the clock hardware instructions to install the clock. Most instructions involve attaching the mechanics to the back side of the record and threading a piece through the center hole.

6. Attach the clock hands and insert the batteries. Set the correct time. Now you're ready to rock!

ADVANCED CRAFTING

Use the ruler (or a protractor, if you have one) to measure out the minutes between the stenciled numbers, then mark them with small painted lines or dots.

Trinkets and Toys Picture Frame

CAUTION

Frame your favorite photo with flair. Look around your room (be sure to check under your bed) for colorful, small trinkets and toys that you can put to crafty good use.

What You Need

Small picture frame with wide, flat border

Small toys, trinkets, game pieces, broken jewelry (or whatever you like)

Hot glue gun

Hot glue

Pom-poms (assorted sizes and colors)

Beaded necklace

Step 2

Step 3

What You Do

1. Gather all the small toys, trinkets, game pieces, and broken jewelry you can find. The more the items vary, the better.

2. Starting at 1 corner, use the hot glue gun to attach items to the picture frame. Ask an adult for help with the hot glue gun, if you need it.

3. Continue gluing items until you have covered all 4 sides of the frame.

4. Fill in any gaps between the items with small pom-poms. Pom-poms are an excellent filler for this project for a few reasons. First, they come in different sizes and colors, which makes the project fun and decorative. Second, they are squishy, which makes them easy to insert between 2 toys that don't meet up perfectly. Third, having something like a pom-pom between the plastic items helps them stay in place by providing another surface for the glue to grab on to.

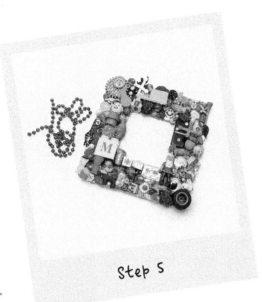

Step 5

Top-Notch Tip
Use craft glue instead of hot glue if you want to be able to rearrange the toys before the glue hardens.

5. Create a fancy border for the frame by gluing a beaded necklace around the outside edges. The beads on many beaded necklaces are connected with string, which makes it easy to cut the necklace to the correct length.

ADVANCED CRAFTING
Create a different look by trimming the frame with toys and trinkets that are various shades of just one color. You might be surprised at how many shades of blue there are!

Glossary

carabiner: Metal spring-loaded loop that is very useful for making things easier to carry (that's why you often see them on key chains). They are also often used by campers for hanging a hammock, or by rock climbers.

decoupage medium: A thick, glue-like liquid traditionally used to decorate objects with paper or used as a protective topcoat. There are different versions, such as matte, shiny, outdoor, or glitter.

furoshiki: A style of cloth used for wrapping gifts in Japan.

jojoba oil: An oil that comes from the jojoba plant used as an additive in many cosmetics.

jump ring: A small circular metal ring that is split at one point and used primarily in jewelry making. The loops come in different sizes, colors, and strengths.

mesh canvas: A plastic, grid-like material used for latch hooking. Also referred to as rug canvas.

multi-surface craft paint: Paint that can be used on various surfaces, such as plastic, wood, and fabric. The bottle will be labeled as such.

pamphlet stitch: A bookbinding technique that changes slightly depending on the number of holes in the spine.

rickrack: A type of sewing trim that looks like a zigzag pattern and comes in various widths and colors.

shibori: A Japanese style of fabric dyeing typically associated with indigo dye and intricate folding patterns. The word *shibori* means to wring, squeeze, or press in Japanese.

sizing: A chemical that is added to most new clothing, especially T-shirts, to prevent them from being marked or stained at the store. It can also prevent them from taking fabric dye.

washi tape: A decorative tape primarily used in paper crafting. It is similar to masking tape in that it is easily removed and reapplied without leaving a sticky residue.

Acknowledgments

Thank you Mary Colgan for helping wrangle me and my run-on sentences. Shout out to my neighborhood Buy Nothing group for more free recycled craft supplies than I could ever ask for.

About the Author

 **Jennifer Perkins** is a creative content designer living in Austin, Texas. She has two crafty kids, one creative husband, and seven fur babies (three cats, two dogs, and two rabbits). When she is not vacuuming pet hair, you can find her at a thrift store, decorating for whatever holiday is coming up next, or color-coordinating her extensive pom-pom collection.

Jennifer comes from a long line of crafters. Her mother, Fredda Perkins, never met a craft supply she didn't like; Jen's sister, Hope Perkins, is an artist; and both of her grandmothers were creative, crocheting, sewing, and making ceramics. Jennifer is keeping things going with her own two children, who both love art, crafts, and other creative endeavors, like cooking and baking.

CPSIA information can be obtained
at www.ICGtesting.com
Printed in the USA
JSHW011041100422
24753JS00002B/3